Keep Calm in Chaos

by Robin Khoury

Adapted from
The Practice of the Presence of God
By Brother Lawrence

A portion of the proceeds from the sale of this book goes to support Little Light Ministries.

To Paula, my precious friend and helper

Copyright © 2010 Robin Khoury

ISBN # 978-0-966-7147-4-6

All rights reserved. No part of this book may be reproduced, stored in a retrieval system, or transmitted in any form without prior consent from the publisher.

www.littlelightpress.com
www.littlelight-ministries.org

Contents

Introduction 5

Part One:
  Conversations with Brother Lawrence 13

Part Two:
  Letters from Brother Lawrence 27

"To get in the habit of talking to God about everything, at first you have to pay really close attention to Him. After a little work building this habit, you will find His love bubbling up inside all the time."

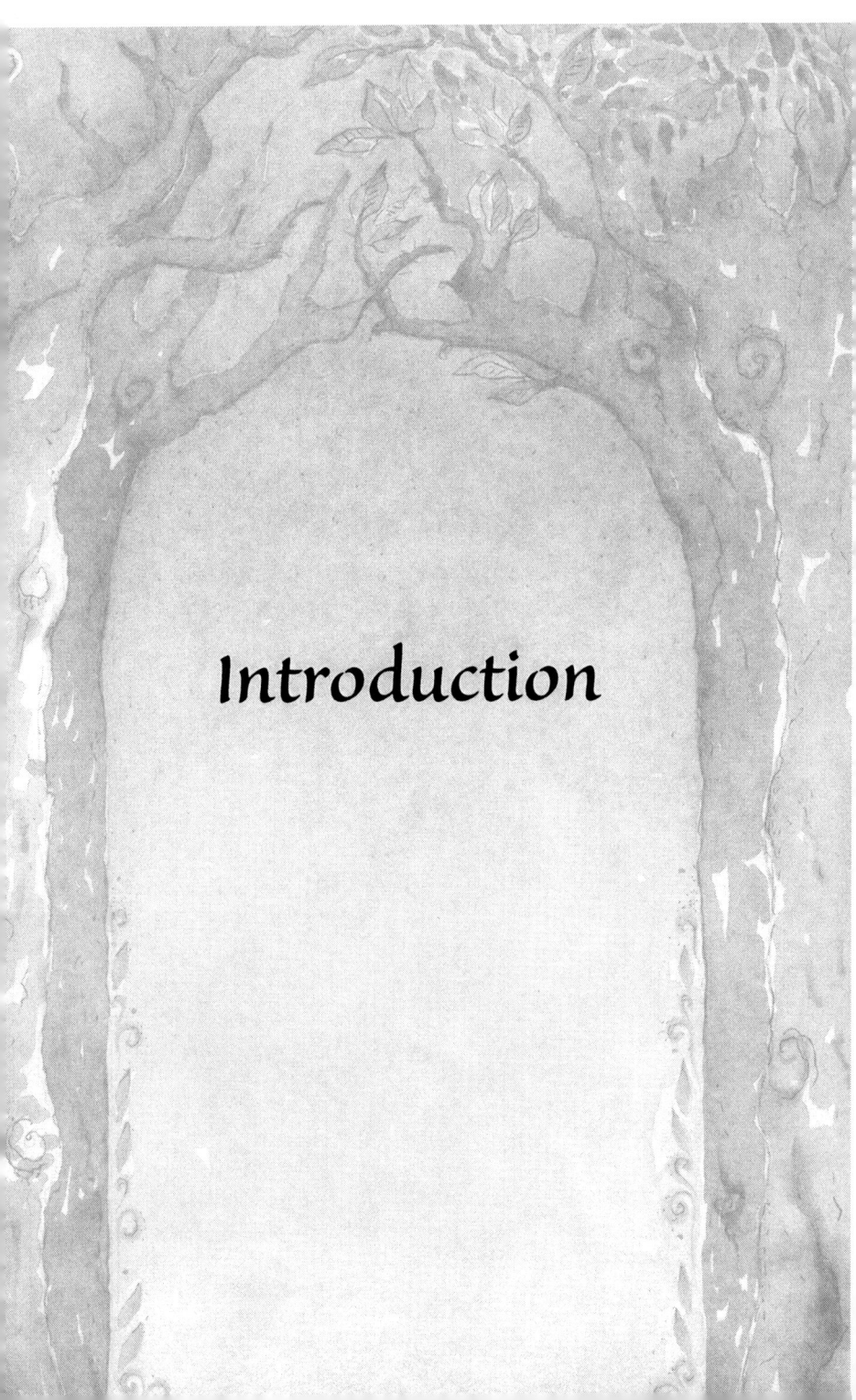

Introduction

"We deal with too much noise, too many disasters, and too much stress."

Stress: A Ticking Time Bomb

Whether you spend your days changing diapers and wiping runny noses, or negotiating Fortune 500 business deals, or coping with life behind prison walls, life is chaotic these days. We deal with too much noise, too many disasters, and too much stress. We have to brace ourselves and work up the nerve to listen to the news. Twenty-first-century living is stressful.

Sometimes we look back at the lives of people in earlier times and pine for "the good old days." We believe that their lives were easier than ours. While that is true in some ways, just think of how a neighborhood grocery store, running water, and cars make our lives easier. That's why my Granny always called them "the good old bad days." She had no desire to go back to the earlier times she had lived through. People living in every era experience their own unique challenges. This brings us to the story of Brother Lawrence, who lived in the Discalced Carmelite Monastery in the late seventeenth century.

A Stressed-Out Monk

Brother Lawrence was stressed out. I know what you are thinking: *How could anyone be stressed out in a monastery? Monks are cloistered—tucked away from the world behind closed doors, bathed in warm candlelight, and surrounded by chanting. How could anyone possibly be stressed out inside a monastery?*

There were several reasons Brother Lawrence was stressed out. Brother Lawrence was a lay monk, and lay monks did all the monastery's daily work. This allowed the educated monks to study and copy scriptures. Brother Lawrence was assigned to work in the kitchen, which he didn't like. He was also getting old—Brother Lawrence was fifty when he joined the order. He was slightly lame from an old war wound and likely in chronic pain. He was also plagued by fear and dread of God. Can you imagine a monk who felt that he was not good enough to receive God's grace? Yes, monastic life was stressful for Brother Lawrence.

Do You Dread Daily Jobs?

Like Brother Lawrence, are you dreading doing jobs that you hate? My mom had a method for dealing with this. Mother hated to iron, and we always had a giant basket of ironing that never got done. It just got bigger and bigger. During the early seventies when polyester was invented, my mom hauled that ironing basket, with all of the clothes in it, out to the trash. She told Daddy that nobody wore that kind of stuff anymore because everything is perma-pressed now. (She didn't want him to be out of style!)

Brother Lawrence's Secret of Stress-Free Living

You know, I hate to admit it, but I once threw away a basket of mending like that. History does repeat itself. But we can't always just throw away what is stressing us out. In the midst of his misery, Brother Lawrence discovered a secret of stress-free living. The secret made so much difference that the other monks noticed. Word spread to folks outside the monastery as well. The change in Brother Lawrence was so great that people came to ask him about it. The Abbot of Beaufort was one of those people. He visited with Brother Lawrence five times and exchanged a series of letters with him. When Brother Lawrence died, the abbot published the conversations and letters under the title *The Practice of the Presence of God by Brother Lawrence*. This book is still in print today and is considered one of the classics of Christian literature.

Brother Lawrence Changes His Mind

So what exactly happened to change Brother Lawrence from upset to peaceful? He finally became so miserable that he decided to totally trust in, lean on, and rely on God. The old monk decided to do everything, from that moment on, out of love for God. He prayed moment by moment. He called this *practicing the presence of God*.

Practicing God's Presence Produces Joy

Brother Lawrence admitted that learning to practice the presence of God was hard work at first. But the hard work produced the reward of continual joy. This joy bubbled over even when he was working hard or was sick or in danger.

Brother Lawrence said,

> *The time of business does not with me differ from the time of prayer, and in the noise and clatter of my kitchen, while several persons are at the same time calling for different things, I possess God in great tranquility as if I were upon my knees at the blessed sacrament.*

If You Are Stressed Out

It has been hundreds of years since Brother Lawrence lived, but his secret is still with us. Are you stressed out? Instead of self-medicating with alcohol and drugs, may I suggest an ancient 17th-century stress buster? Practice the presence of God. Talk to Him moment by moment as you do the dirty jobs on your list. To find out more, read on. Now you can read *The Practice of the Presence of God* in everyday, modern English.

Why Another Version of the Original?

There are many good reasons to read original versions of old books. I am not a big fan of dumbed-down books of any kind. But there is also a reality that must be faced: Most people in our century don't have great vocabularies, and many people have reading problems. As I read through the version of *The Practice of the Presence of God* that I owned, I kept my dictionary by my side. Most folks won't take the time to do that.

Paraphrases: Good News for Busy People

I suppose we can employ the same argument for using paraphrases of the Bible. I remember when I was in the sixth grade and the deacon at my church gave me a copy of *The Good News Bible*. I was ecstatic. I still have that Bible. It is only one in my extensive collection, but I still enjoy reading it from time to time. As I read and reread *The Practice of the Presence of God* while writing *The Grumpy Monk*, a children's book about Brother Lawrence, I kept thinking, "How would I say that?"

Keep Calm in Chaos: The Practice of the Presence of God in Everyday English

So I looked up the big words, shortened the sentences, and edited a few repetitious parts. The end result is *The Practice of the Presence of God* that anyone with an eighth-grade reading level can enjoy. I pray that *Keep Calm in Chaos* will bring Brother Lawrence and his discovery of contentment through Christ into our generation.

Part One:
Conversations with Brother Lawrence

"The miracle of renewed life caused me to think about how God personally takes care of the world and His creatures in it."

Brother Lawrence's Christian Testimony

It was winter. I noticed a bare tree, stripped of its leaves. I started thinking about the fact that in the spring the leaves would come back and flowers and fruit would appear. The miracle of renewed life caused me to think about how God personally takes care of the world and His creatures in it. These thoughts made a permanent mark on my soul and cut me loose from worldly ideas. That day God lit a passion in me for Himself that still burns brightly now, forty years later.

Lessons and Struggles

After I became a believer in Christ, my life was still not easy. I struggled with daily living and wrong spiritual ideas. I spent years as an errand boy for Mr. Fieubert, an accountant. This was hard work for me because a war wound had left me partially lame. I am a big, clumsy guy.

I joined the monastery so I could suffer for my awkwardness and the sins I had committed. I wanted to sacrifice my life and pleasures to God. This didn't turn out as I expected, though, because in doing this I found great joy and satisfaction. I believe that we should bring ourselves into a sense of God's presence by talking to Him all the time. It is shameful to stop talking to God just to think about unimportant things.

Three Tips to Help You Practice the Presence of God

Feed and nourish your soul with thoughts about God. This brings great joy. Live your life in faith. It is sad that people amuse themselves with devotional plans rather than living in faith. Living in faith helps us grow in Christ.

Give yourself completely to God in both physical and spiritual things. Look for satisfaction only in doing what He wants you to do, whether He leads you by suffering or comfort. We must be faithful in prayer even when it seems dry, things don't make sense, or we are upset. This is when God tests our love for Him. We should submit ourselves to Him even more during these times, and we will grow even more.

Thoughts About Sin

Don't be surprised at the misery and sin going on in the world. In fact, considering the evil nature of people, it is surprising that there is not more wickedness. Pray for evil people. God can take care of their bad conduct if and when He pleases. Don't worry about these things.

In order to give ourselves over totally to God's will, we must sort out all our emotions and desires that get mixed up in our physical and spiritual lives. To those who truly seek Him, God will reveal the things that need to be repented of.

When I finally understood God's grace, I decided to make the love of God the reason for all my actions. This decision made me very happy. I came to the point where I was happy to pick up a piece of straw from the ground for the love of God, seeking Him only—nothing else, not even His gifts.

Dealing with Fear

For a long time I was worried about going to hell. Nobody could talk me out of this. I was troubled about this for four years, which caused me to be upset and depressed. Finally I realized that my fears were caused by a lack of faith. I had placed my sins between myself and God because I believed that I did not deserve salvation. Finally I resolved this by reasoning with myself in this way: "I lived my life loving God with all my heart. I have lived only for Him, no matter what happens to me. Whether I am lost or saved, I will keep on loving Him. At the end of my life at least I will know this: I have loved God with all my heart." After this realization I felt perfect freedom and continual joy.

How to Start Practicing the Presence of God

To get in the habit of talking to God about everything, at first you have to pay really close attention to Him. After a little work building this habit, you will find His love bubbling up inside all the time.

After living so many days in pleasantness while practicing the presence of God, I expect that I will one day experience suffering. I don't worry about this, though. I believe that the Lord will give me the strength to bear whatever He brings into my life.

When an opportunity arises for me to do good, I pray, "Lord, I can't do this unless You enable me." Always after this prayer I receive more than enough strength.

How to Stop Worrying About Failure

When you fail, simply confess your wrong, saying to God, "I will always do it wrong if You leave me to myself. You must keep me from falling and fix what is wrong." If you don't fail, thank God, knowing that your strength comes from Him.

We should talk to God simply, frankly, and plainly. We should ask Him to help us with everything that happens to us, right when it happens. God has never failed to help me the many times I have asked.

Sometimes I have to go to Burgundy to buy meat for the monastery. I hate doing this because, for one thing, I'm not good at bargaining. Also, my lame leg causes me to have to scoot on my bottom over a bunch of barrels to get on the boat. I don't worry about this humiliation, though. I just remind myself that this is God's business, not mine.

This is the same way I deal with my dislike for my work in the kitchen. After I decided to do everything in the kitchen for the love of God, I prayed all the time for grace to do my work well. After this I found everything easy for the next fifteen years that I worked there.

Prayer Life

With me, set times of prayer are not different than other times. I am expected by my superior to set aside prayer times, but I don't want these times. I would rather pray all the time, even when I am busiest. I don't need someone to stand over me and make sure I say my prayers. My whole reason for living is to love God in all things. In the beginning I had trouble with my mind wandering during scheduled prayer times. I realized that I was not going to be able to concentrate in a legalistic devotional hour like many do. I was able to meditate for a while, but afterward my mind wandered, and I didn't know where the time went.

I do feel a need to confess, however, because I'm very sensitive to my sins and shortcomings. I don't let them discourage me. I just confess them to God and continue living in love with Him. Disobedience to God begins in the mind. We should reject useless thoughts as soon as we recognize them and return to our communion with God.

When I'm troubled and depressed, I don't consult anybody. I have faith that God is with me, and I do everything to please Him, come what may.

The Place of Self-Denial

All self-denial is useless. The best way to have a conversation with God is to do all things out of love for Him. Our only business is to love and delight ourselves in God. All kinds of self-denial do not erase even one sin. We should expect Jesus Christ to forgive our sins and not worry. We should love Him with all our hearts. I have experienced the greatest pleasures and pains while loving God. That's why I don't worry about anything and am not afraid. My only desire is that I will not disappoint God.

Do Everything for the Love of God

The basis for my spiritual life is a great respect for and faith in God. My main goal is to reject any other thought and do everything for the love of God. If it happens that I forget and go a long time without thinking about God, I don't worry about it. I just ask God to forgive me and return to Him with even greater trust.

Grace

The trust we put in God honors Him and draws down much grace. I have so often received God's help in many different circumstances that I am not anxious when I have things to do. I don't worry about it. I just find in God the strength needed for the task.

Desiring God

When I become too busy to think about God, He sends a fresh thought of Himself into my soul. This mental impression excites me so that I can hardly contain myself. I am closer to God while I am working than I am during my set-aside prayer times.

Someday I might have great physical or mental pain. But the worst thing that could happen would be to lose my fellowship with God. God is good and will not leave us. He will give us the strength to bear whatever evil He permits to touch our lives. I am not afraid. I don't try to talk to anybody about my problems. Every time I do, I come away with more doubts and fears than I had before. I am not afraid of danger, and I find that acceptance of God's will is a perfect guide for my actions. When we have problems, we should just turn to Jesus Christ for help and protection. We should ask for His favor and mercy, and He will help us.

Things That Get in the Way of Growth

Many people don't grow in their Christian lives because they get stuck in rituals and neglect the love of God. This is obvious by the way they live and is the reason we don't see more goodness in the world. A person does not need to understand art or science to understand God. He only needs a heart determined to live for Him and love Him only.

Ask God for Help

We must reject everything that does not lead us toward God. We should understand that God is with us and in us every moment so we can get used to talking to Him all the time. We must ask Him to show us what He wants us to do. Then we must also ask Him to help us do the things He has shown us. We should offer them to Him before we do them and thank Him when we are finished. As we carry on this conversation with God, we also praise, adore, and love Him for His infinite goodness and perfection.

God Never Fails; People Do

God never fails in giving His grace. At times I have forgotten to ask God for help or have let my mind wander out of His presence. Our growth in Christ does not depend on our changing ourselves but on doing for God what we usually do for ourselves. It is sad to see how many people start doing all kinds of imperfect work for God for their own selfish reasons. I do my work purely for the love of God.

We must put our whole trust in God and totally surrender ourselves to Him. Because we love the Lord, we shouldn't get tired of doing little things. God doesn't look at the greatness of the work but at the love with which it is performed. We shouldn't be surprised when we fail. If we keep doing these things, we will form a habit, which will naturally produce good works in us, and we will be delighted.

The Christian life consists of faith, hope, and love. Through these we become one with the will of God and become the people God has planned for us to be. Nothing else matters. All things are possible to him who believes. They are easier for those who hope and love, and they are easier still for those who keep on practicing these virtues.

Self-Examination

We should set a goal to become the most perfect worshipers of God that we can in this life because that is what we will be doing in heaven. When we start walking with God, we should take an honest look at ourselves. We should find ourselves disgusting and sinful and not worthy to call ourselves Christians. After taking a long, hard look at ourselves, we shouldn't be surprised that bad things happen to us because of other people who are just like us. The more godliness a person desires, the more he is dependent on God's grace.

Brother Lawrence's Personal Experience

After God changed my attitude, the other monks asked how I got such a sense of the presence of God. When I came to the monastery, in the beginning I spent my hours appointed for prayer thinking of God. I did this rather than studying reasoning or elaborate meditations. After I filled my mind with the sense of the presence of God, I went to work in the kitchen. I spent all my time before and after work in prayer. As I began my work, I said, "O my God, You are with me, and in obedience to You I start my work. Please give me grace to stay in Your presence. Please help me do well. I offer this work to You as well as my love." I continued this conversation with my Maker all the time I was working.

When I finished, I evaluated my work. If I did well, I thanked God. If not, I asked forgiveness and set my mind right. By getting up after I fall and by renewing faith and love, now it is as hard for me not to think of God as it was to get used to it in the beginning.

"We should set a goal to become the most perfect worshipers of God that we can in this life because that is what we will be doing in heaven."

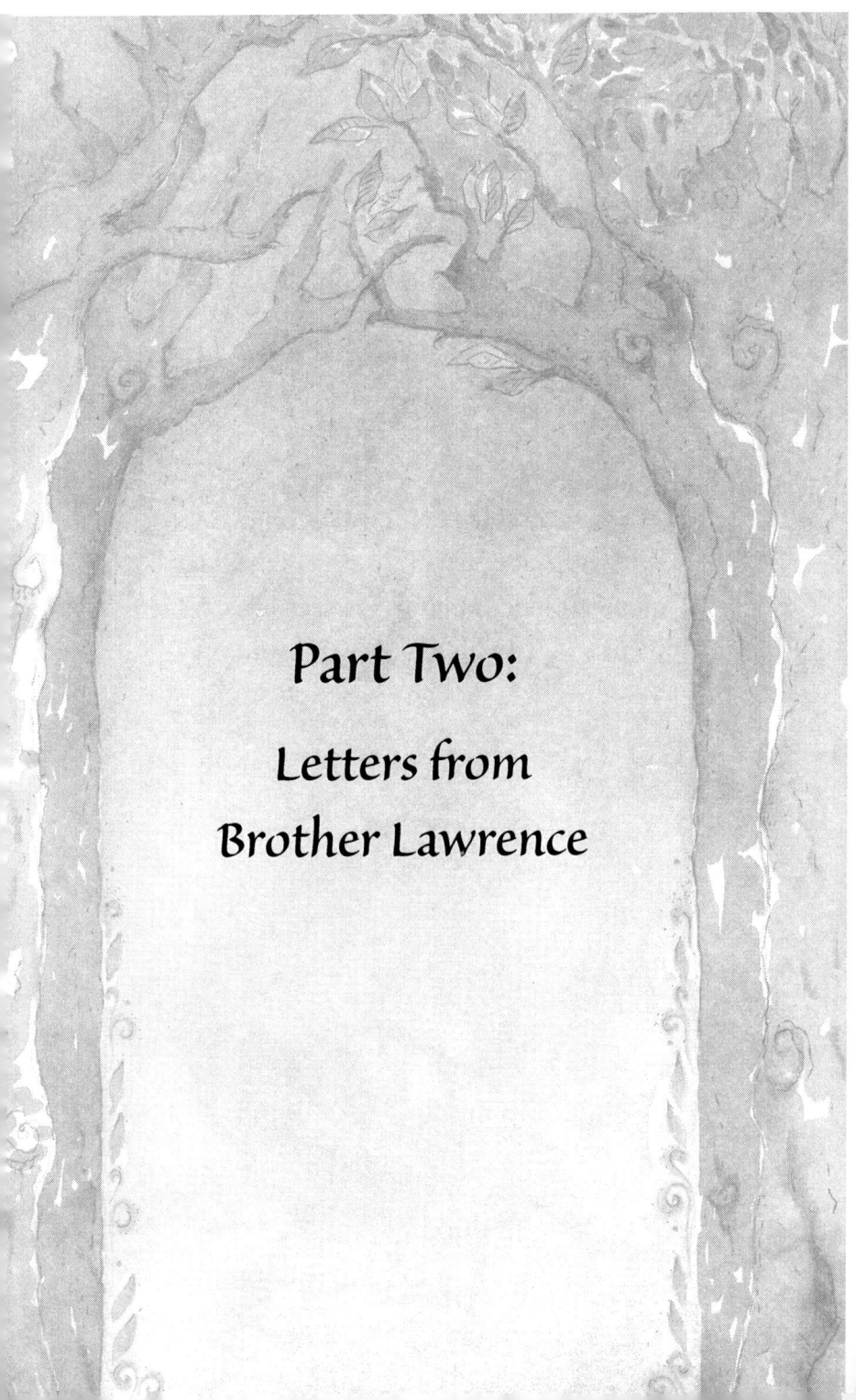

Part Two:

Letters from Brother Lawrence

"When I decided that I would continue to believe as long as I lived, even in the midst of my troubles, I found myself changed all at once. My troubled soul became peaceful."

First Letter

I Gave Myself to God

Through the years I have found lots of different spiritual things to do. I decided that all of these things were confusing me and not getting me where I wanted to be with God. What I wanted was to be wholly His. This prompted me to give my whole self over to Him. After doing this, He took away my sins. I put aside everything that wasn't of Him, and I began to live as if there was nobody else in the world except Him and me.

Focus on God

Sometimes I thought of myself as a poor criminal at the mercy of his judge. At other times I saw Him as my Father, as my God. I worshiped Him as often as I could, keeping my mind in His holy presence. I brought this back to my mind whenever it wandered away from Him. This was really painful, but I kept on even though it was hard. I didn't worry about it when my mind wandered; I just re-focused it as soon as I realized what had happened. I did this all the time, including in my quiet times with God. I focused my mind on God every hour and every minute, even when I was really busy. I drove every thought out of my mind that interrupted my thoughts of God.

We Can't Do Anything Without Him

I haven't always done this perfectly, but whenever I have done it, I have found it to be very helpful. I know God showed me these things by His goodness and mercy. None of us, especially me, can do anything without Him. When we keep ourselves in God's presence and keep Him foremost in our minds, this not only keeps us from doing wrong, but it also deepens our friendship with Him. This is one way God strengthens us, too.

Repetition Helps Form Habits

By doing these things over and over, they become habits, and the presence of God becomes natural to us. Would you thank Him now with me for His great goodness to me? I can't put into words how great God is and how many wonderful things He has done for me, a miserable sinner. May all things praise Him! Amen.

Second Letter

Give Up Everything Except Love for God

In my spiritual life I have not followed all the methods that others follow. I found that things like that discouraged me. This was why, when I became a monk, I decided to give myself up to God. I found this the best way to thank Him for loving me. I decided at that moment to give up everything else except my love for Him.

Faith Alone Satisfies

For the first year after I decided this, during my devotional times I thought about death, hell, judgment, and my sins. I did this for several years. During the rest of the day I thought about the presence of God, even when I was busy. Finally I tried doing this during my devotional time as well, which gave me great joy. This also gave me such respect for God that faith alone was able to satisfy me then.

This was how it began, but I must admit that my first ten years were full of suffering. I worried constantly that I wasn't devoted enough to God, and my past sins were always present in my mind. I felt guilty about the undeserved blessings that God gave me. During this time I fell away from God and reached back for Him many times. It seemed like the whole world and everybody in it, even God, was against me. When I decided that I would continue to believe as long as I lived, even in the midst of my troubles, I found myself changed all at once. My troubled soul became peaceful.

Walk Simply in Faith with Humility and Love

Ever since then, I have walked before God simply in faith with humility and love. I work hard at doing and thinking only those things that please Him. I can't really explain the peace in my soul now. I am not worried or anxious about my spiritual state. My only desire is to do the will of God. I am so determined to do this that I won't even pick up a piece of straw unless I feel He wants me to. The only reason I do anything is out of love for Him.

I have stopped using all formal prayers in my private devotions. The only thing I keep on doing is to stay in His holy presence. I pay attention to Him and think of Him fondly. I have a habitual, silent, and secret conversation in my soul with God. This makes me overflow with joy sometimes. Sometimes I get so joyful that I have to settle myself down so that others won't notice.

Abandon Yourself into God's Hands

In short, I am totally convinced that my soul has been saved for the last thirty years. I am the most wretched of men, full of sores and sins. I have committed all sorts of crimes against Jesus, my King. When I realize it, I confess to Him all my wickedness. I ask His forgiveness. I abandon myself into His hands that He may do what He wishes with me. My King does not punish me but wraps His loving arms around me, brings me to His table to eat, serves me with His own hands, and gives me the keys to His treasures.

The Lord talks to me and delights in me all the time in a thousand different ways. He treats me like His favorite child. I feel this way when I am in His holy presence.

Pay Attention to God All the Time

The main way I do this is by simply paying attention to God all the time. This state of being is like a baby at his mother's breast. That's why I call this sweet feeling that I get "the bosom of God." If I get away from this because of sickness or busyness, my memories of the sweet experiences there draw me back. But I would rather you focus on my unworthiness rather than the great favors God has done for me.

Present Yourself to God as Stone to a Sculptor

My set times of prayer have become a continuation of being in His presence. Sometimes I see myself in His presence as a stone before a sculptor. I present myself to Him as this. I want Him to carve His perfect image in my soul.

At other times I feel my spirit and soul lift itself up without any effort on my part. It stays there as if in a place of rest. Some people say that I have just dreamed this up. I can't stand it when people say this because when I enjoy God like this, I don't want anything but what He wants. So if I am just dreaming these things, then it is God's job to take it away. My only desire is to be wholly devoted to Him.

Third Letter

God Is Kind

Our God is extremely kind and knows all about our wants. I have always known that God will eventually bring you to the end of yourself. He will come in His own time and when you least expect it. Hope in Him more than ever. Thank Him with me for the favors He does you, especially for the strength and patience He gives you when things aren't going well. He takes care of you. Comfort yourself with Him, and be thankful to Him.

God Sends Affliction to Cause Us to Trust Him

God sends affliction to cause us to trust Him and put away worldliness. Put all your trust in Him, and think of Him as often as you can, especially when you are in danger. A little lifting of your heart to God, a thought of Him, and inward worship are good enough. Even short prayers please God. They are like a sword in your hand. They give you courage in danger. Think of

God as often as you can. You have to get used to this little by little. Nobody will notice it, and nothing could be easier.

Fourth Letter

Learn from the Example of Others

In this letter, I want to tell you how one of the other monks benefits from practicing the presence of God. We can learn from him.

For the last forty years since joining the monastery, his decision has been to be in touch with God all the time. He doesn't do, say, or think anything that will displease Him. He does this purely for the love of God because He deserves more than all the love we can give Him.

Practicing the Presence of God Brings Joy

He has gotten so used to living in God's presence that he gets help from this practice all the time. He has been so joyful for the last thirty years that he has to hide it sometimes to keep from disturbing the other monks.

If he gets away from God's presence for a while, God draws him back to Himself. This usually happens when he is most engaged in his outward business. He pays attention when God does this by lifting his heart to God, by thinking a meek or fond thought of God, or by expressing a statement of affection such as, "O God, here I am, totally devoted to You. Make me what You want me to be."

When he does this, he feels like God is happy with this and rests in the center of his soul. These experiences give him such assurance that he is incapable of doubting God at all. Just imagine what satisfaction he gets out of this treasure. He doesn't have to worry or search for peace with God. He has it.

We Are Happy with Too Little

My friend complains a lot about our blindness. He says that we are so pitiful because we are happy with so little. God has unlimited treasure to give us, and we are happy with a few minutes of devotional time that are soon passed. We are so blind that we stop the flow of His grace. But when God finds a soul full of lively faith, He pours into it His grace and favor to overflowing. In fact, He floods that soul with His goodness.

Stop Putting Boundaries Around God's Grace

Yes, we often stop the flow of grace by the little boundaries we put around it. Let's stop doing this! Let's make way for God's grace and redeem the lost time because we don't know how much we have left. We must get ready for the day that we will die because all of us are going to die.

In a Storm, Wake Up the Lord

We must take a hard look at ourselves. Time is passing by, and there is no time to waste. Our souls are at stake. You cannot stand still in your spiritual development; that is going backward. Those who have the wind of the Holy Spirit at their backs go forward even while they are sleeping. If our souls are tossed with winds and storms, we must wake up the Lord who is sleeping in our boat, and He will calm the sea.

I have taken the liberty to tell you these experiences so that you can compare them to your own. They will serve to rekindle your love for God if it should ever cool off (though that would be awful). We can grow by the example of my friend, who is not known by the world but is known to God. I will pray for you. Please pray for me right now.

Fifth Letter

Empty Your Heart of Everything But God

I know that if a person is going to practice the presence of God, the heart must be empty of everything else because God possesses the heart alone. God cannot possess it completely and do what He wants to do there unless it has been left vacant for Him.

Nowhere is there a sweeter or more delightful life than that of a constant conversation with God. The only people who understand it are those who have experienced it. That being said, I hope that you don't do it for that reason. We should not seek pleasure for ourselves in our practice; we should do it out of love, as God would have us do.

If I were a preacher, I would preach the practice of the presence of God above everything else. If I were in charge, I would advise everybody in the world to do this. That's how much I believe this.

We Need the Grace and Presence of God

If we only knew how much we need the grace and presence of God, we would never lose sight of Him, even for a minute. Please decide firmly to never forget Him again and to spend the rest of your life in His presence because of your love for Him—even if that means doing without everything else if that is His will.

Start working hard at this, and if you do it like you should, you can be sure that you will soon notice a difference. I will help you with my prayers, as poor as they are.

Sixth Letter

Keep God in the Center of Your Soul

I can't imagine how Christians can have a satisfying spiritual life without the practice of the presence of God. I keep God in the center of my soul as much as I can. While I am with Him, I'm not afraid of anything. Doing this doesn't make me tired. It is good to deprive your body sometimes, though, of many of the little pleasures that we enjoy so much. If you want to be totally devoted to God, you should be willing to put Him first.

I'm not advocating any sort of violent self-denial. We serve God in a holy freedom. We must do our jobs faithfully, without grumbling, returning our minds gently to God whenever we realize that we have wandered.

Put Your Whole Trust in God

It is necessary to put our whole trust in God, laying aside all other cares and even some forms of personal devotions. Although these things can be very good, they are the means to an end. If by practicing the presence of God we are with Him who is our end, it is then useless to return to meaningless devotional practices. We can keep exchanging love with Him, persevering in His holy presence. We can do this by sometimes praising, sometimes thanking, and doing many other things that our spirits will invent.

Don't Be Discouraged

Don't be discouraged by the fact that this doesn't come naturally. You must force yourself to do it. At first you might think it is a waste of time, but you must go on and decide to keep on doing it until you die.

Seventh Letter

God Is Nearer Than You Know

I feel very sorry for you. I think it would be better for you to turn your business over to someone else now and spend the rest of your life worshiping God. He doesn't require great things of us—a little remembrance of Him here, a little adoration, a little prayer for grace, an offering of our sufferings to Him, a little thanks for everything He has done for you. Lift up your heart to Him, even while you are eating and when you are with people. God appreciates all the little ways that you remember Him during the course of your day. You don't need to shout and cry for Him. He is nearer than we know.

Talk to God in Your Heart

It is not necessary to always be at church to be with God. We can have a loving conversation with Him in our hearts. Anybody can do this. God knows us.

We don't have much time left to live. Be brave. Let us live and die with God. Even suffering will be sweet and pleasant to us while we are with Him. Without Him, the greatest pleasures would be a cruel punishment. May He be blessed forevermore.

Don't Be Obsessed with Rules

Get used to worshiping Him little by little. Beg for Him to help you, and offer Him your heart from time to time in the midst of your busy days, even every moment. Don't be obsessed with rules and certain forms of devotion. Believe in God with confidence and humility. I am praying for you.

Eighth Letter

Ask God to Help You Practice His Presence

About your wandering thoughts in prayer—you aren't the only one who has this problem. Our minds wander naturally. Our will is in charge of our other mental processes. Use it to carry them to God. When we first start practicing the presence of God, our minds have a lot of bad habits to overcome. It is natural for your mind to draw you to worldly things against your will.

When Your Mind Wanders, Don't Get Upset

I believe one remedy for this is to confess our faults and humble ourselves before God. I don't advise that you talk too much and give big speeches to God in prayer when your mind has wandered. Instead, hold yourself in prayer like a paralyzed beggar at a rich man's gate. Decide to keep your mind in the presence of the Lord. Don't get upset when your mind wanders; this will distract you even more. Just decide to get back in the presence of God peacefully. If you keep doing this, God will help you.

Keep Your Mind in God's Presence

One way to keep your mind focused at prayer time is to keep it from wandering too far at other times. If you keep your mind completely in the presence of God moment by moment, then it will be easier to keep your mind calm when you are praying. I have already told you the advantages of practicing the presence of God. Let us take this seriously and pray for each other.

Ninth Letter

Don't Try to Grow Too Fast

Don't try to become holy all at once. It doesn't happen that way. We need to think that our only reason for living is to please God. Everything else is foolishness. I have lived about forty years as a monk. Have I employed these years in loving and serving God who called me to do this? I am ashamed when I think back on all the great things God has done for me and never stops doing for me. I have not made the best use of them, and I haven't grown very much.

Turn Away from Everything That Is Not of God

God in His mercy has given us a little more time to live. Let us begin in earnest and redeem the lost time. Let's return to the Father of mercies, who is always ready to receive us lovingly. Let's turn away from everything that is not of Him, for the love of Him. He deserves even more than this.

Put All Your Trust in God

Let's think of Him without stopping. Let us put all our trust in Him. I know that we will reap the rewards of this by receiving the abundance of His grace. With this we can do all things, and without it we can't do anything but sin.

Pray for God's Help

We can't escape the dangers that are everywhere without the constant help of God. We must pray for Him to help us all the time. How can we pray to Him without being with Him? How can we be with Him without thinking of Him often? How can we think of Him without building a habit?

It sounds like I am always saying the same thing. I admit it. This is the best way I know. It is the one that I use, and I advise everybody to do it. We must know before we can love. In order to know God, we must think often of Him. And when we come to love Him, then we will also think often of Him, for our hearts will be with our treasure. Think about this.

Tenth Letter

God Will Never Fail You

I am very happy about the trust that you have in God. I pray that He will increase it more and more. We can't place too much trust in such a good and faithful Friend, who will never fail us in this world or in the next.

Ask God to Help You Overcome Grief

When you lose someone you love, put all your trust in God. He will soon fill the empty space in your life with another friend or loved one to take the place of the one you have lost. We must leave this up to God. There is always the possibility that you were too attached to this person. We ought to love our friends and relatives, but not more than we love God.

Don't Wander Away from God

Remember my recommendation to think about God often—by day, by night, in your business, and in your pleasure. He is always near you and with you; don't wander away from Him. You wouldn't leave a friend alone who came to visit you, so why do you leave God alone?

Adore God All the Time

Don't forget Him. Think about Him often, adore Him all the time, and live and die with Him. This is the glorious job of the Christian. If we don't know how to do it, then we must learn. I will try to help you with my prayers.

Eleventh Letter

Ask God for Strength to Bear Pain

I don't pray that you will get out of your pain, but I do pray that God will give you strength and patience to bear it as long as He pleases. Comfort yourself with Him who holds you fastened to the cross. He will take you down when He sees fit. Those who suffer with Christ are happy. Suffer like this, and ask Him for strength to endure as much or as long as He thinks necessary for you.

Don't Be Distressed in Sickness

Worldly people don't understand this. It is easy to see the difference in them when they suffer. They think of sickness as a pain from nature and not as a favor from God. When they see it only in this light, it is no wonder that they find only grief and distress in it. But those who consider sickness as coming from the hand of God find sweetness and comfort.

God Holds Your Cure in His Hands

I wish you could find it in your heart to believe that sometimes God is nearer to us in sickness than in health. Don't rely on any other physician. According to my understanding, He is holding your cure in His hands. Put all your trust in Him. You will find that many times we hurt ourselves by putting more confidence in medicine and doctors than in God.

Whatever remedies you take, they will only help you as much as He allows. When pain comes from God, only He can cure them. Sometimes God sends diseases of the body to cure those of the soul. Comfort yourself with the Sovereign Doctor of the soul and body.

Be Satisfied with Your Condition

Be satisfied with whatever condition the Lord places you in. No matter how happy you think I am, I envy you. It would be heaven for me to suffer with my God. The greatest pleasures would be hell to me if I had to try to enjoy them without Him. All my comfort and hope would be to suffer something for God. In a little while, I will be going to Him. What comforts me in this life is that I now see Him by faith. I see Him in a way that might make me say, "I don't believe. I *see*. I feel what faith has taught me. In the assurance and practice of faith, I will live and die with Him."

Stay in God's Presence and Believe in Him

Keep on staying in God's presence and believing in Him. It is the only healing for your sickness. I will ask Him to be with you. Let me know if I can help you in any way.

Eleventh Letter

Offer God Your Pain

If we were in the habit of practicing the presence of God, we would not get so many diseases. God often allows us to suffer to give us a reason to cry out to Him. Be brave. Offer Him your pain all the time. Pray to Him for strength to endure it. Adore Him in your illness. Offer yourself to Him from time to time. Ask Him like a little child asks his father to help you accept His holy will. I will pray for you, too.

Faith Will Not Fail You

God has many ways of drawing us to Himself. Sometimes He hides Himself from us, but faith alone should be our support. Faith will not fail us in our time of need. Faith in God should be our foundation.

I don't know what God is going to do with me. I am always happy. Everybody else in the world is unhappy and suffering, and I who deserve the worst punishment feel so much joy that I can barely contain myself. I wish I could ask God to let me share in your sufferings. But I know my weakness. If He left me one moment to myself, I would be the most wretched man alive. But I don't know how He could leave me alone. I know He never leaves us; we leave Him. Let us live and die in His presence. Please pray for me as I am praying for you.

Thirteenth Letter

God Allows Those He Loves to Suffer

It hurts me to know you have been suffering for so long. The only thing that comforts me in this is knowing that this is proof of how much God loves you. If you think of it like this, it will be easier to bear. It is my opinion that you should stop all medical treatment and put yourself wholly in the hands of God. Maybe He is only waiting on you to completely trust Him for your cure. Since none of the medical cures have helped you so far and you are getting sicker, it would not be tempting God to abandon yourself to His hands and expect Him to heal you.

Ask God for Strength and Endure

In my last letter I told you that God sometimes allows bodily diseases to cure the sicknesses of the soul. Be brave, then, and ask God not to deliver you from your pain but to give you strength to endure it in love as long as He pleases.

God Is the Father of the Afflicted

Such prayers aren't easy to say, but they are sweet to God and those who know Him. Love sweetens pain. When one loves God, he suffers for His sake with joy and courage. I encourage you to comfort yourself with Him, who is the only Physician for all our maladies. He is the Father of the afflicted, always ready to help us. He loves us infinitely more than we can imagine. Love Him back, and don't seek help other places. I hope you will get it soon. I will help you with my prayers.

Fourteenth Letter

Pray for Strength in Suffering

I thank the Lord for having relieved your suffering some. I have been close to death many times but never was as satisfied as then. I didn't pray for healing, but I prayed for strength to suffer with courage, humility, and love. Ah, how sweet it is to suffer with God! However great your sufferings are, receive them with love.

Make Your Heart a Church

If we are to enjoy the peace of heaven in this life, we must get used to a familiar, humble, loving conversation with Him. We must keep our spirits focused on Him all the time. We must make our hearts a church in which to adore Him moment by moment. We must watch over ourselves all the time, making sure that we don't say or think anything that might displease

Him. When we keep our minds occupied like this, suffering will become full of comfort and hope.

God Gives Grace to Those Who Ask

It's hard to do this in the beginning. We have to do it in faith. Even though it is hard, we also know that we can do all things through Christ who strengthens us. God never refuses to give His grace to those who ask. Knock and keep on knocking, and I assure you that He will open the door for you in due time. He will give you all at once what He has kept back all these years. Please pray for me as I am praying for you. I hope to see Him soon.

Fifteenth Letter

God Does Everything for Our Good

God knows what is best for us. Everything He does is for our good. If we really understood how much He loves us, we would always be ready to receive everything from Him, the bitter and the sweet. It only seems like we can't stand the worst things that happen if we see them in the wrong light. When we see them as handed to us from God, when we know that it is our loving Father who distresses us, suffering loses its bitterness and becomes helpful.

Love God Equally in Pleasure and Pain

Let everything we do help us to know God. The more you know Him, the more you want to know Him. The more you know Him, the more you will love Him. We should love Him equally in pleasure and in pain.

We should not love God merely for the kind favors that He does for us. All these things do not bring us as near to Him as one simple act of faith. He should be within you if you have invited Him. Don't look for Him other places. If we don't love God above all else, are we not rude? Do we not deserve blame if we keep ourselves busy with things that don't make Him happy and even offend Him? These worldly things will one day prove to be very costly to our souls.

Give God All Your Heart

Let's begin to be earnestly devoted to Him. Let's get everything else out of our hearts. He wants to completely own them. Beg Him to give you favor. If we do our part, we will soon see the change in our hearts that we want so badly. I can't thank Him enough for the peace of mind that He has given you. I pray that in His mercy He will let me see Him in a few days. Let's pray for each other.

Prayer from Robin Khoury:

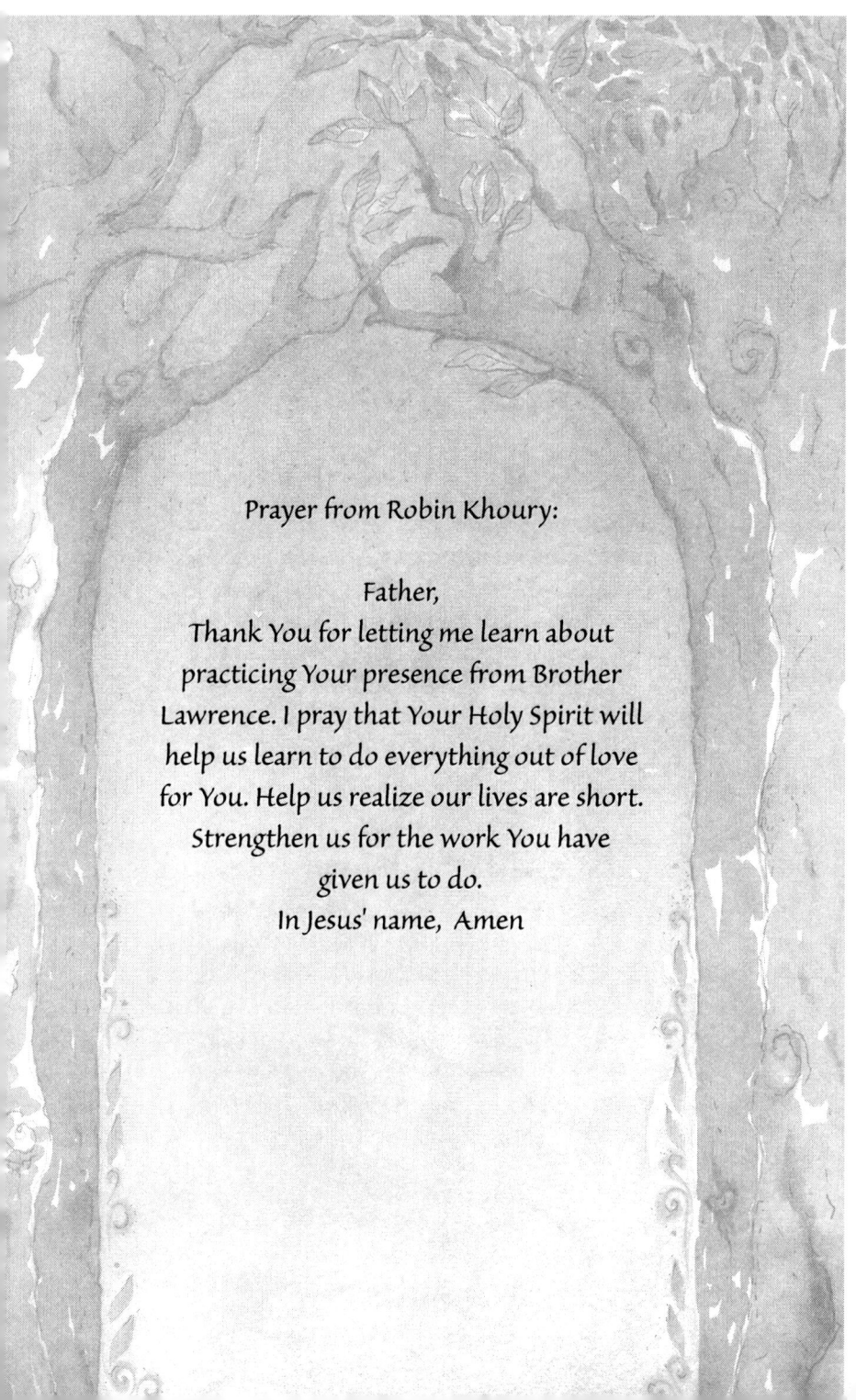

Father,
Thank You for letting me learn about practicing Your presence from Brother Lawrence. I pray that Your Holy Spirit will help us learn to do everything out of love for You. Help us realize our lives are short. Strengthen us for the work You have given us to do.
In Jesus' name, Amen

About the Author

Robin Khoury is a wife, mother of two sons, and former homeschooling mom. She and her husband E.J. enjoy entrepreneurial adventures, gardening, and cooking Middle Eastern food. The Khourys take turns hosting and traveling to visit their large Christian Arab family in Israel. Robin Khoury is a popular speaker at churches and women's events. You can contact Robin at www.robinkhoury.com.

About Little Light Ministries, Inc

A portion of the proceeds of all Little Light Press books goes to support Little Light Ministries. The domestic mission of Little Light Ministries is to evangelize, educate, and encourage women who have been in prison or jail in Oklahoma and ministers to the children of these women. You can find out more about the different projects of Little Light Ministries, Inc., at www.littlelight-ministries.org.

Also by Robin Khoury

Looking for a practical way to teach children about living life in Christ? ***The Grumpy Monk*** by Robin Khoury is the story of how one grumpy monk got a hug from God that changed his life. Miss Robin retells for children the Christian classic *The Practice of the Presence of God* by Brother Lawrence. Illustrated in watercolor and colored pencil by Polish artist Agnieszka Korfanty.

Every time BiC (Babe in Christ) thinks about baptism, his tummy tickles just like he is on a roller coaster. Can Disciple Dan, Mr. Owl, and Pastor Windy help BiC learn what baptism mean? Can BiC learn to trust God with his fears? ***BiC's Baptism***, a picture book for elementary children, reviews the meaning of baptism by immersion for children while delighting children with the award-winning artwork of Kevin Scott Collier.

Where else can you find a storybook, coloring book, activity book, and keepsake all rolled into one? ***Answers for New Christians*** is all that and much more. ***Answers*** is 72 pages packed with salvation information and assurance for those who have already been saved. The keepsake section in the back helps children remember their salvation with places for parents, family members, and loved ones to write blessings, prayers, and memories. Artwork by homeschooling dad Stuart Corley.

CPSIA information can be obtained at www.ICGtesting.com
Printed in the USA
BVOW07s0136290814

364698BV00001B/29/P